the journey is long

poetry for the desert of life

ISBN: 9798327500037
Imprint: Independently published

written to my younger self,
and to all my fellow travelers
on the healing journey

.

Sweet Fellow Traveler,

I am immensely grateful you have chosen to read this book. I prayed it would find you. Writing these poems has been incredibly therapeutic for me. Publishing them is an invitation for you to accompany me on this journey. By reading The Journey is Long, I feel like you are inviting me to join you on your journey. Together, we can share our experiences of pain, grief, healing, and triumph. I share my experiences in the upcoming pages, and perhaps one day, I will have the privilege of hearing your stories.

I hope some of my experiences resonate with you and make you feel seen, understood, inspired, encouraged, or simply less alone. There's no right or wrong way to read this collection of poems. You can read it traditionally, chapter by chapter, or choose a page at random that interests you. Let's embark on this meaningfully rich adventure ahead.

Warm Regard,
SaLeena

seasons

creation   **11 - 20**

the fall   **21 - 30**

the tomb   **31 - 58**

resurrection   **59 - 73**

resources   **78 - 83**

season one

creation

be productive

prove your worth

busy has no time

get first place

no less than A's

average is never fine

- socially acceptable generational curses

feed me feed me

my ego screams

tell me i'm good

i need to be seen

a pat on the back

a bouquet of roses after the show

keep the compliments coming

you're feeding me too slow

- hunger of a wounded ego

the sound hurts my ears

the clanging is loud

no patience or love

drowned in the applause of the crowd

- nothing without love

if i sleep with a Bible under my head

if i eat the pages

if i glue them to my eyes

i have not become any more like Jesus

- religious striving

better to die loved and sick
than healthy and alone
we focus on miracles of healing
more than caring for our home

even if you walk on water
you could die and go to hell
ministering to large crowds
but never loving people well

- misplaced priorities

gifts can be a burden to bare
most people can't see past the bow
what's really on the inside
will anyone take time to really know

it almost makes you invisible
but it lights up their face
you introduce yourself as a gift
so no one can take your place

you get smaller and smaller
until you forget the truth too
who you are is the real gift
it's not just what you do

carrying trash

walking over treasure

- spiritual blindness

"the moment i found out we were going to have you, my heart was so full of love for you. before i knew you'd be beautiful, smart, talented, or kind, my heart was full of love for you."

- it's bittersweet to think i spent 33 years thinking i had to earn his love

i was once climbing a mountain

feeling pretty good

people were affirming

i was doing what i should

i realized in horror

when i almost reached the top

these mountains aren't really real

i slammed on the brakes to stop

i got down and started walking

through the valley and through the snow

watching the other climbers climb

faux mountains but they didn't know

boots, hats, and gloves

cheering one another on

Lord help these poor souls

give them courage to move beyond

- ladder of achievement

season two

the fall

i never said anything at first
because it wasn't that big of a deal
when it happened a second time
i thought maybe i'm crazy this isn't real

it got to be too much
i was in too deep to get out now
i wanted to reach for help
no one ever slowed down to teach me how

you are just a girl
no one would believe
it must have been your fault
just like the story of adam and eve

you'll lose everything you love
i wish now i hadn't believed the lie
but i was so convinced
it will end if i just comply

- fawn trauma response

where were you when i needed help
i didn't know i was supposed to yell
i guess it wouldn't have mattered much
because you weren't around to tell

love me angry

love me broken

or don't love me at all

the weight of my secrets
is drowning my soul
it's time to let go
it's time to be whole

layer by layer
healing takes time
it's messy and awkward
like a poem with no rhyme

valleys and mountains
the journey is long
but it takes a while to unpack
all that was done wrong

be gentle and slow
give lots of grace
for the road less traveled
is a very sacred space

i'm singing for the ones that never told
about the bad things that happened
when they were young
but now they're old
it's not your fault what happened to you
when you were just a girl
and you didn't even have a clue

here's a poem for my sisters
God heal the pain of my sisters

i'm singing for the ones who grew up alone
without a mother or father
no love were they ever shown
it's not your fault what happened to you
i know you needed the love
so you did what you had to do

here's a poem for my sisters
God heal the pain of my sisters...

…to the women out there who are feeling alone
to the one who feels lost
with no place to call home
caught up in the world with one million fears
at night you sit alone just you and your tears
full of regret for the pain you can't forget
guilt, shame got you down
girl lift up your head
the Father's got a crown for you to wear
He put a light in you for you to share
don't be afraid when the night comes
people try to put you down don't let them
you're my sister, you're a queen
girl i hope that you know
you're God's daughter you're a star now show it

here's a poem for my sisters
God heal the pain of my sisters

- saleena bishop and kristin mallory

lock up the books
they grow her too tall
i know she can run
but i make her crawl
learn to be normal
learn to stay small
don't rock the boat
tradition might fall

maybe you'll think less of me
i'm not afraid anymore
down from this golden pedestal
the veil He rent and tore

break me out of this glass house
the one i helped build myself
i'm not a role, i'm a human
please don't sit me on a shelf

- breaking expectations

drip

i tried to fix the leak

drip, drip

i called the plumber

voicemail

drip, drip, drip

i laid on the cool tile

embracing the sounds of

things i cannot change

drip, drip, drip, drip

- tired

how long can

you fly without gas

season three

the tomb

i kept apologizing for taking too much time

you kept reassuring me

i was the reason you came

you wanted to be here for me

you weren't in a hurry

you said don't be ashamed

with tissues you let me cry

i wasn't used to people who listen

your ears mended my wings

i can't explain

grateful

- purpose promise experience

on the ground or in the air

a bird is a bird

anywhere

- seasons of rest

they evolve over time

they grow and shrink

it's all part of it

why are we afraid of change

it's not supposed to stay the same

they are a blessing sent for a season

for years or for a day

cherish them

- adult friendships

looking to belong
heart guarded against rejection
fear says there's no seat
until you finally reach perfection

love builds you a chair
with gratitude, you build one too
belonging saves the seat
for all those coming after you

no mean girls here in sight
only sisterhood allowed
everyone's valued here
for those in the back
let's say it loud

- belonging > rejection

before we were close

i threw away your journal

when i found it in some donated books

not in the trash can

in the dumpster

so no one could read it

- sweet friends

i saw you

hidden in the background of my picture

i saw the look on your face

the care and compassion in your eyes

the camera discreetly exposed your love

when you were unaware

and no one was looking

- deep love

when i started my business
you were the first one i told
later that day
i found a gift on my doorstep
celebrating my achievement

- thoughtful friends

tell me goodbye
if i ever meant anything to you
please hug me tight
if i ever meant anything to you

i've been hurt and rejected
so many times
left without word or warning
like i wasn't worth a dime

finally someone cared
enough to gently let me know
it healed me inside
even though they were letting me go

- the power of a kind goodbye

to get me a tiny gift

you almost missed your flight

with years of meaning behind it

your love never shined so bright

it made me feel so seen

you remembered what i said

after 20 years you gave me

what i thought only existed in my head

- precious treasures from paris

when i can't breathe
you give me oxygen
you are a bridge to calm
when you hold me
i feel the arms of Jesus

- loving relationships

the day it all went down
i didn't know what else to do
i left you to fend for yourself
too much pain for me to get through

every day since then
i regret the choice i made
i promise i'll never leave you again
the next time we part will be the grave

- healing disassociation

i understand why you left me

i would have left me too

if only one of us could live

i'm glad that you chose you

imagine my surprise

you came back to find me

i'm glad to get to know you

healing together with the Almighty

- healing disassociation

brush your hair slowly

be gentle with yourself

you learn to love by being

take time to nurture the garden of your soul

- self-care

you were my first gift

how am i nurturing you

how am i protecting you

how am i loving God's daughter

\- learning to love yourself

now i see the real reason people don't tell
when you tell, they sentence you
want to put you straight in hell

now i see the real reason people don't tell
when you tell, they silence you
when you're already living in hell

just move on, let go, forgive
quit holding on to the past and just live
well i'm sorry if you heard those words
i know it only made things worse

let the water of the word wash over you
it can heal you, cleanse you, and make you new
it can heal you in your deepest parts
invite Jesus in your heart, that's where it starts…

…bring the dark things of your soul

let them come to light

it's ok, you're safe now if you want to cry

just don't carry the weight alone

we believe you

no one here's going to throw a stone

you weren't made to carry

the weight on your own

bring it to the light

when you do, you'll see

it's not as hard as you thought it'd be

bring it to the light

now i know the reason people don't tell

but you weren't made to live in hell

come up to the light

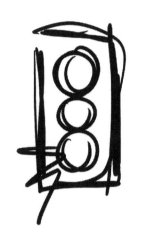

feelings aren't the enemy

they are simply a sign

a guide for the path

when given curiosity and time

what if all i have is a lot of anger
sadness and shame
what if all i have is a broken heart
and little pieces of pain

would you take them as an offering
if i brought them to you
turning ugly into beauty
isn't that something that you do

i'm bringing my offering
i'm bringing all my ugly things
and someday when they turn to gold
i'll lay them at your feet
as a crown for you to hold

- ugly offerings

dear anger,

i'd like to reintroduce myself

when i was young i believed a lie about you

that you were useless, evil and bad

that you would never help

no matter how much of you there was

it never made a difference

i guess that's when we broke up

life happened

we went our separate ways

it turns out, you were the very thing i needed

in many situations, you would have saved me

can you forgive me

i want to make peace with you

so you don't have to keep popping up

in unexpected places

i'd really like to get to know you

maybe someday we could even be friends

- sorry

you held me when i was in labor

when i was ugly

and couldn't carry the weight of the pain

you were my shelter

my defender

a safe place

your words of encouragement

lit up my path

and gave me the strength to keep going

- hope

i'm only halfway there

i think i'm gonna die

healing is no joke

most people don't and i see why

keep going

don't stop now

you're on the right track

who knew it would be so hard

finding courage to look back

- therapy

one day

i pray you feel

safe enough to tell

how you fell and got back up

and made it back

from hell

you don't hang your dirty clothes
with your clean clothes
so it is with us
wounds leave us feeling broken and dirty
feeling like we don't belong with the clean clothes

this can lead to bad decisions
because who cares about
getting a stained shirt dirty
the pile of shame and condemnation grow
all part of satan's plan to keep us
in the dirty clothes pile

you sin because you're hurting
then you're hurting because you've sinned
so the cycle goes, seeming to never end

know you're never too stained
to be beyond redemption
the love of Christ is more powerful
than anything you've done
or that's been done to you

- grace

season four

resurrection

the smell of a wounded heart
permeates through the waves
the shark senses the fragrance
as predators, they start to crave

the innocent and naive
fall easy prey into their hands
with grooming traps they weave
their deception secures the bands

freed with gentle truth
bathed in love and grace sweet oil
healed and redeemed
now carries the aroma of a royal

- wounded is not your identity

a second to break

a lifetime of repair

but what if we aren't so fragile

and strength is hidden in despair

what if the journey is just beginning

with a ticket stamped in pain

there is a beautiful life ahead

if you are brave enough to board the train

up in my attic
i found an old bracelet
i made as a child
together
my nine year old self and i
said to one another
'i made it'

rivers of pain

hidden in the heart

drawn up with gentle questions

safe to flow freely

trickle as tears

- therapy

never stop reaching up

to heal is better than revenge

life is a canvas

brushes in the hand of free will

joy chooses the colors

desire decides what to paint

stop looking at the paintings of others

paint what makes your heart smile

don't like what you've painted, repaint it

someone punched a hole through

the canvas, repair it

when you die show the master artist your work

- finding your purpose

sometimes we worry

about disappointing God

finding our purpose

why were we created

we don't want to take a wrong step

but in the beginning, God never made a

tightrope for us to walk on

He created a garden for us to explore

right where you are

is where you're meant to be

never hurried

fully present

living truly free

let the stonethrowers rage

watch their kingdoms crumble

build with every rock

a castle for the humble

when you feel loved, safe, and secure
the fruits of your life are
joy, peace, and confidence

jealousy, envy, fear, and competition
are fruits of feeling unloved & insecure

friend you are loved

i can never go back
to being a slave of busy
once befriending rest

when i let you see my pain
you looked at me with love
no judgment or rejection
such a gift could only come from above

i thought i was bad
i thought surely you'd be scared
but your soft eyes let me know
now the burden would be shared

- eyes of Jesus

the devil says become something to be loved

Christ says come let me love you

while you're becoming

you were already waiting on the other side

silently cheering for me

take the first step

when i did, you couldn't help yourself

you ran to my rescue

not to save me from the pain

to hold my hand and walk with me

because you knew

the journey is long

it was hard, but it was good

and she lived happily ever after...

the end

xoxo

enjoy your journey

Sweet Fellow Traveler,

I want to honor you for your strength. This journey of inner healing is a treacherous one. Sometimes we get weary, tired of crying, feeling alone, and wondering when will the pain end. I've been there too.

I'm not quite fully on the other side, but I can see now, I'm not nearly as fragile as I once thought I was. Partnering with the Holy Spirit and taking each step day by day has been the best decision of my life. Sure, there may still be days I feel like quitting, giving up, wishing I could turn back. But I see now, how God creates us to be strong. How he made us to co-labor with him and together we can get through anything.

We can do hard things. I'm so thankful for all the anointed people the Lord appointed along my path: guides, therapists, life coaches, friends, and family. Remember, you are not alone. There are many of us travelers out here. I pray you keep going on your journey. It is a long one. I believe you and I believe in you.

Warm Regard,
SaLeena

Resources

*These are a small list of the companies and ministries I've personally worked with along my journey. I am not a paid representative of any of them. I want to clarify the poems in this book do not reflect the opinions of these organizations. I simply wanted to pass along my personal recommendations. I can't speak highly enough of each of these places and their heart to see people walk in healing and wholeness. They are listed in the order I was introduced to them:

*I realize many of these references are for Ohioans, but I pray you see help wherever you live. It's not weak to ask for help, it's actually very courageous. If you seek help but it doesn't feel like a good fit, keep looking. Don't give up.

The Purpose Promise

The Purpose Promise provides a safe place for those in transition, both in their career and in life. The truly gifted leaders, compassionately offer a soft place to land. They listen and give guidance along the path. They help you gain clarity for your next steps. **www.purposepromise.org**

Dove House Ministries

I was 33 when I went on my first silent retreat. This Christian ministry provides a beautiful, peaceful, and healing experience. Through silence and solitude, I was able to hear the Lord clearly and find comfort in His presence. **www.dovehouseministries.org**

Currahee Center -

With anointed life coaches and licensed counselors, The Currahee Center offers a variety of healing services. Listening, teaching, deliverance, communion and prayer are just a couple of the ministries they offer to break off the past and to give you tools for your future success.
www.curraheecenter.org

Thrive Point Counseling

This was the first place my husband was ever willing to go to counseling. Our counselor was so kind, wise, and gracious. At times a referee, and sometimes a coach. She helped bridge the gap between us and teach us healthy tools we still use to this day to strengthen our marriage.
www.thrivepoint.com

Intact Counseling

The first time in my life I was able to share all the messy, dirty, and unwanted experiences of my life and receive warm positive regard in return, was at Intact Counseling. They provide a very sacred, safe space to unpack the challenges of life. Their state-licensed mental health professionals provide confidentiality and guidance with no judgment or shame.

www.intactcounseling.com

Sonscape Retreats

For pastors and their wives, or really anyone in church leadership, I would recommend Sonscape Retreats. To be around likeminded ministers from all over, helps you to feel understood. Their anointed retreat leaders help you to process the difficulties of ministry and care for you as a person, not just a position. The mountains of Colorado add to the beauty of the experience. **www.sonscaperetreats.org**

Book Recommendations

The Emotionally Healthy Leader

By: Pete Scazzaro

Unraveled

By: Deanna Lorea

The Night is Normal

By: Alicia Britt Chole

Connect with me on Instagram

@slowdownlovewell